This Tracker Belongs to:

Start Date:

End Date:

What's Happening Today _____________

Track your moods or situations on a daily basis so that you can keep track of changes and be aware of shifts and their outcomes. It doesn't have to take long!

My Health	My Work	My Friends
My Children	My Diet	My Dreams
My Goals	My Finances	My Partner
My Family	My Life	My Mental Health

What's Happening Today __________

Track your moods or situations on a daily basis so that you can keep track of changes and be aware of shifts and their outcomes. It doesn't have to take long!

My Health	My Work	My Friends
My Children	My Diet	My Dreams
My Goals	My Finances	My Partner
My Family	My Life	My Mental Health

What's Happening Today __________

Track your moods or situations on a daily basis so that you can keep track of changes and be aware of shifts and their outcomes. It doesn't have to take long!

My Health	My Work	My Friends

My Children	My Diet	My Dreams

My Goals	My Finances	My Partner

My Family	My Life	My Mental Health

What's Happening Today __________

Track your moods or situations on a daily basis so that you can keep track of changes and be aware of shifts and their outcomes. It doesn't have to take long!

My Health	My Work	My Friends
My Children	My Diet	My Dreams
My Goals	My Finances	My Partner
My Family	My Life	My Mental Health

What's Happening Today _________

Track your moods or situations on a daily basis so that you can keep track of changes and be aware of shifts and their outcomes. It doesn't have to take long!

My Health	My Work	My Friends
My Children	My Diet	My Dreams
My Goals	My Finances	My Partner
My Family	My Life	My Mental Health

What's Happening Today ____________

Track your moods or situations on a daily basis so that you can keep track of changes
and be aware of shifts and their outcomes. It doesn't have to take long!

My Health	My Work	My Friends
My Children	**My Diet**	**My Dreams**
My Goals	**My Finances**	**My Partner**
My Family	**My Life**	**My Mental Health**

What's Happening Today _______________

Track your moods or situations on a daily basis so that you can keep track of changes and be aware of shifts and their outcomes. It doesn't have to take long!

My Health	My Work	My Friends
My Children	My Diet	My Dreams
My Goals	My Finances	My Partner
My Family	My Life	My Mental Health

What's Happening Today _____________

Track your moods or situations on a daily basis so that you can keep track of changes
and be aware of shifts and their outcomes. It doesn't have to take long!

My Health	My Work	My Friends
My Children	**My Diet**	**My Dreams**
My Goals	**My Finances**	**My Partner**
My Family	**My Life**	**My Mental Health**

What's Happening Today _____________

My Health	My Work	My Friends
My Children	**My Diet**	**My Dreams**
My Goals	**My Finances**	**My Partner**
My Family	**My Life**	**My Mental Health**

What's Happening Today __________

Track your moods or situations on a daily basis so that you can keep track of changes and be aware of shifts and their outcomes. It doesn't have to take long!

My Health	**My Work**	**My Friends**
My Children	**My Diet**	**My Dreams**
My Goals	**My Finances**	**My Partner**
My Family	**My Life**	**My Mental Health**

What's Happening Today __________

Track your moods or situations on a daily basis so that you can keep track of changes and be aware of shifts and their outcomes. It doesn't have to take long!

My Health	My Work	My Friends
My Children	My Diet	My Dreams
My Goals	My Finances	My Partner
My Family	My Life	My Mental Health

What's Happening Today _______________

Track your moods or situations on a daily basis so that you can keep track of changes
and be aware of shifts and their outcomes. It doesn't have to take long!

My Health	My Work	My Friends

My Children	My Diet	My Dreams

My Goals	My Finances	My Partner

My Family	My Life	My Mental Health

What's Happening Today __________

Track your moods or situations on a daily basis so that you can keep track of changes
and be aware of shifts and their outcomes. It doesn't have to take long!

My Health	My Work	My Friends
My Children	My Diet	My Dreams
My Goals	My Finances	My Partner
My Family	My Life	My Mental Health

What's Happening Today _____________

Track your moods or situations on a daily basis so that you can keep track of changes
and be aware of shifts and their outcomes. It doesn't have to take long!

My Health	My Work	My Friends

My Children	My Diet	My Dreams

My Goals	My Finances	My Partner

My Family	My Life	My Mental Health

What's Happening Today ___________

Track your moods or situations on a daily basis so that you can keep track of changes and be aware of shifts and their outcomes. It doesn't have to take long!

My Health	My Work	My Friends

My Children	My Diet	My Dreams

My Goals	My Finances	My Partner

My Family	My Life	My Mental Health

What's Happening Today ____________

Track your moods or situations on a daily basis so that you can keep track of changes and be aware of shifts and their outcomes. It doesn't have to take long!

My Health	My Work	My Friends

My Children	My Diet	My Dreams

My Goals	My Finances	My Partner

My Family	My Life	My Mental Health

What's Happening Today _____________

Track your moods or situations on a daily basis so that you can keep track of changes and be aware of shifts and their outcomes. It doesn't have to take long!

My Health	My Work	My Friends

My Children	My Diet	My Dreams

My Goals	My Finances	My Partner

My Family	My Life	My Mental Health

What's Happening Today __________

Track your moods or situations on a daily basis so that you can keep track of changes
and be aware of shifts and their outcomes. It doesn't have to take long!

My Health	My Work	My Friends
My Children	My Diet	My Dreams
My Goals	My Finances	My Partner
My Family	My Life	My Mental Health

What's Happening Today __________

Track your moods or situations on a daily basis so that you can keep track of changes
and be aware of shifts and their outcomes. It doesn't have to take long!

My Health	My Work	My Friends
My Children	My Diet	My Dreams
My Goals	My Finances	My Partner
My Family	My Life	My Mental Health

What's Happening Today _____________

Track your moods or situations on a daily basis so that you can keep track of changes and be aware of shifts and their outcomes. It doesn't have to take long!

My Health	My Work	My Friends
My Children	**My Diet**	**My Dreams**
My Goals	**My Finances**	**My Partner**
My Family	**My Life**	**My Mental Health**

What's Happening Today __________

Track your moods or situations on a daily basis so that you can keep track of changes
and be aware of shifts and their outcomes. It doesn't have to take long!

My Health	My Work	My Friends
My Children	My Diet	My Dreams
My Goals	My Finances	My Partner
My Family	My Life	My Mental Health

What's Happening Today __________

Track your moods or situations on a daily basis so that you can keep track of changes
and be aware of shifts and their outcomes. It doesn't have to take long!

My Health	My Work	My Friends

My Children	My Diet	My Dreams

My Goals	My Finances	My Partner

My Family	My Life	My Mental Health

What's Happening Today _____________

Track your moods or situations on a daily basis so that you can keep track of changes
and be aware of shifts and their outcomes. It doesn't have to take long!

My Health	My Work	My Friends

My Children	My Diet	My Dreams

My Goals	My Finances	My Partner

My Family	My Life	My Mental Health

What's Happening Today _____________

Track your moods or situations on a daily basis so that you can keep track of changes and be aware of shifts and their outcomes. It doesn't have to take long!

My Health	My Work	My Friends
My Children	**My Diet**	**My Dreams**
My Goals	**My Finances**	**My Partner**
My Family	**My Life**	**My Mental Health**

What's Happening Today __________

Track your moods or situations on a daily basis so that you can keep track of changes
and be aware of shifts and their outcomes. It doesn't have to take long!

My Health	My Work	My Friends
My Children	My Diet	My Dreams
My Goals	My Finances	My Partner
My Family	My Life	My Mental Health

What's Happening Today __________

Track your moods or situations on a daily basis so that you can keep track of changes and be aware of shifts and their outcomes. It doesn't have to take long!

My Health	My Work	My Friends
My Children	My Diet	My Dreams
My Goals	My Finances	My Partner
My Family	My Life	My Mental Health

What's Happening Today __________

Track your moods or situations on a daily basis so that you can keep track of changes
and be aware of shifts and their outcomes. It doesn't have to take long!

My Health	My Work	My Friends
My Children	My Diet	My Dreams
My Goals	My Finances	My Partner
My Family	My Life	My Mental Health

What's Happening Today ___________

Track your moods or situations on a daily basis so that you can keep track of changes
and be aware of shifts and their outcomes. It doesn't have to take long!

My Health	My Work	My Friends
My Children	My Diet	My Dreams
My Goals	My Finances	My Partner
My Family	My Life	My Mental Health

What's Happening Today __________

Track your moods or situations on a daily basis so that you can keep track of changes
and be aware of shifts and their outcomes. It doesn't have to take long!

My Health	My Work	My Friends
My Children	My Diet	My Dreams
My Goals	My Finances	My Partner
My Family	My Life	My Mental Health

What's Happening Today ___________

Track your moods or situations on a daily basis so that you can keep track of changes
and be aware of shifts and their outcomes. It doesn't have to take long!

My Health	My Work	My Friends
My Children	My Diet	My Dreams
My Goals	My Finances	My Partner
My Family	My Life	My Mental Health

What's Happening Today __________

Track your moods or situations on a daily basis so that you can keep track of changes
and be aware of shifts and their outcomes. It doesn't have to take long!

My Health	My Work	My Friends
My Children	**My Diet**	**My Dreams**
My Goals	**My Finances**	**My Partner**
My Family	**My Life**	**My Mental Health**

What's Happening Today _____________

Track your moods or situations on a daily basis so that you can keep track of changes and be aware of shifts and their outcomes. It doesn't have to take long!

My Health	My Work	My Friends
My Children	My Diet	My Dreams
My Goals	My Finances	My Partner
My Family	My Life	My Mental Health

What's Happening Today _______________

Track your moods or situations on a daily basis so that you can keep track of changes and be aware of shifts and their outcomes. It doesn't have to take long!

My Health	My Work	My Friends

My Children	My Diet	My Dreams

My Goals	My Finances	My Partner

My Family	My Life	My Mental Health

What's Happening Today ___________

Track your moods or situations on a daily basis so that you can keep track of changes and be aware of shifts and their outcomes. It doesn't have to take long!

My Health	My Work	My Friends
My Children	My Diet	My Dreams
My Goals	My Finances	My Partner
My Family	My Life	My Mental Health

What's Happening Today _______________

Track your moods or situations on a daily basis so that you can keep track of changes
and be aware of shifts and their outcomes. It doesn't have to take long!

My Health	My Work	My Friends

My Children	My Diet	My Dreams

My Goals	My Finances	My Partner

My Family	My Life	My Mental Health

What's Happening Today __________

Track your moods or situations on a daily basis so that you can keep track of changes and be aware of shifts and their outcomes. It doesn't have to take long!

My Health	My Work	My Friends

My Children	My Diet	My Dreams

My Goals	My Finances	My Partner

My Family	My Life	My Mental Health

What's Happening Today __________

Track your moods or situations on a daily basis so that you can keep track of changes and be aware of shifts and their outcomes. It doesn't have to take long!

My Health	**My Work**	**My Friends**
My Children	**My Diet**	**My Dreams**
My Goals	**My Finances**	**My Partner**
My Family	**My Life**	**My Mental Health**

What's Happening Today _______________

Track your moods or situations on a daily basis so that you can keep track of changes
and be aware of shifts and their outcomes. It doesn't have to take long!

My Health	My Work	My Friends
My Children	My Diet	My Dreams
My Goals	My Finances	My Partner
My Family	My Life	My Mental Health

What's Happening Today __________

Track your moods or situations on a daily basis so that you can keep track of changes and be aware of shifts and their outcomes. It doesn't have to take long!

My Health	**My Work**	**My Friends**
My Children	**My Diet**	**My Dreams**
My Goals	**My Finances**	**My Partner**
My Family	**My Life**	**My Mental Health**

What's Happening Today _______________

Track your moods or situations on a daily basis so that you can keep track of changes
and be aware of shifts and their outcomes. It doesn't have to take long!

My Health	My Work	My Friends
My Children	**My Diet**	**My Dreams**
My Goals	**My Finances**	**My Partner**
My Family	**My Life**	**My Mental Health**

What's Happening Today _____________

Track your moods or situations on a daily basis so that you can keep track of changes
and be aware of shifts and their outcomes. It doesn't have to take long!

My Health	My Work	My Friends
My Children	My Diet	My Dreams
My Goals	My Finances	My Partner
My Family	My Life	My Mental Health

What's Happening Today __________

Track your moods or situations on a daily basis so that you can keep track of changes and be aware of shifts and their outcomes. It doesn't have to take long!

My Health	My Work	My Friends
My Children	My Diet	My Dreams
My Goals	My Finances	My Partner
My Family	My Life	My Mental Health

What's Happening Today _____________

Track your moods or situations on a daily basis so that you can keep track of changes
and be aware of shifts and their outcomes. It doesn't have to take long!

My Health	My Work	My Friends

My Children	My Diet	My Dreams

My Goals	My Finances	My Partner

My Family	My Life	My Mental Health

What's Happening Today ___________

Track your moods or situations on a daily basis so that you can keep track of changes
and be aware of shifts and their outcomes. It doesn't have to take long!

My Health	My Work	My Friends

My Children	My Diet	My Dreams

My Goals	My Finances	My Partner

My Family	My Life	My Mental Health

What's Happening Today _______________

Track your moods or situations on a daily basis so that you can keep track of changes
and be aware of shifts and their outcomes. It doesn't have to take long!

My Health	My Work	My Friends

My Children	My Diet	My Dreams

My Goals	My Finances	My Partner

My Family	My Life	My Mental Health

What's Happening Today _____________

Track your moods or situations on a daily basis so that you can keep track of changes
and be aware of shifts and their outcomes. It doesn't have to take long!

My Health	My Work	My Friends
My Children	My Diet	My Dreams
My Goals	My Finances	My Partner
My Family	My Life	My Mental Health

What's Happening Today _______________

Track your moods or situations on a daily basis so that you can keep track of changes and be aware of shifts and their outcomes. It doesn't have to take long!

My Health	My Work	My Friends

My Children	My Diet	My Dreams

My Goals	My Finances	My Partner

My Family	My Life	My Mental Health

What's Happening Today _____________

Track your moods or situations on a daily basis so that you can keep track of changes
and be aware of shifts and their outcomes. It doesn't have to take long!

My Health	My Work	My Friends
My Children	**My Diet**	**My Dreams**
My Goals	**My Finances**	**My Partner**
My Family	**My Life**	**My Mental Health**

What's Happening Today _______________

Track your moods or situations on a daily basis so that you can keep track of changes and be aware of shifts and their outcomes. It doesn't have to take long!

My Health

My Work

My Friends

My Children

My Diet

My Dreams

My Goals

My Finances

My Partner

My Family

My Life

My Mental Health

What's Happening Today _______________

Track your moods or situations on a daily basis so that you can keep track of changes and be aware of shifts and their outcomes. It doesn't have to take long!

My Health	My Work	My Friends
My Children	My Diet	My Dreams
My Goals	My Finances	My Partner
My Family	My Life	My Mental Health

What's Happening Today _____________

Track your moods or situations on a daily basis so that you can keep track of changes and be aware of shifts and their outcomes. It doesn't have to take long!

My Health	My Work	My Friends

My Children	My Diet	My Dreams

My Goals	My Finances	My Partner

My Family	My Life	My Mental Health

What's Happening Today ___________

Track your moods or situations on a daily basis so that you can keep track of changes and be aware of shifts and their outcomes. It doesn't have to take long!

My Health	My Work	My Friends
My Children	My Diet	My Dreams
My Goals	My Finances	My Partner
My Family	My Life	My Mental Health

What's Happening Today _______________

Track your moods or situations on a daily basis so that you can keep track of changes
and be aware of shifts and their outcomes. It doesn't have to take long!

My Health	My Work	My Friends

My Children	My Diet	My Dreams

My Goals	My Finances	My Partner

My Family	My Life	My Mental Health

What's Happening Today __________

Track your moods or situations on a daily basis so that you can keep track of changes
and be aware of shifts and their outcomes. It doesn't have to take long!

My Health	My Work	My Friends
My Children	My Diet	My Dreams
My Goals	My Finances	My Partner
My Family	My Life	My Mental Health

What's Happening Today __________

Track your moods or situations on a daily basis so that you can keep track of changes and be aware of shifts and their outcomes. It doesn't have to take long!

My Health	My Work	My Friends
My Children	**My Diet**	**My Dreams**
My Goals	**My Finances**	**My Partner**
My Family	**My Life**	**My Mental Health**

What's Happening Today ___________

Track your moods or situations on a daily basis so that you can keep track of changes and be aware of shifts and their outcomes. It doesn't have to take long!

My Health	My Work	My Friends

My Children	My Diet	My Dreams

My Goals	My Finances	My Partner

My Family	My Life	My Mental Health

What's Happening Today ______________

Track your moods or situations on a daily basis so that you can keep track of changes and be aware of shifts and their outcomes. It doesn't have to take long!

My Health

My Work

My Friends

My Children

My Diet

My Dreams

My Goals

My Finances

My Partner

My Family

My Life

My Mental Health

What's Happening Today _______________

Track your moods or situations on a daily basis so that you can keep track of changes
and be aware of shifts and their outcomes. It doesn't have to take long!

My Health	My Work	My Friends
My Children	**My Diet**	**My Dreams**
My Goals	**My Finances**	**My Partner**
My Family	**My Life**	**My Mental Health**

What's Happening Today _____________

Track your moods or situations on a daily basis so that you can keep track of changes
and be aware of shifts and their outcomes. It doesn't have to take long!

My Health	My Work	My Friends
My Children	My Diet	My Dreams
My Goals	My Finances	My Partner
My Family	My Life	My Mental Health

What's Happening Today ___________

Track your moods or situations on a daily basis so that you can keep track of changes and be aware of shifts and their outcomes. It doesn't have to take long!

My Health	My Work	My Friends

My Children	My Diet	My Dreams

My Goals	My Finances	My Partner

My Family	My Life	My Mental Health

What's Happening Today _______________

Track your moods or situations on a daily basis so that you can keep track of changes and be aware of shifts and their outcomes. It doesn't have to take long!

My Health	My Work	My Friends

My Children	My Diet	My Dreams

My Goals	My Finances	My Partner

My Family	My Life	My Mental Health

What's Happening Today __________

Track your moods or situations on a daily basis so that you can keep track of changes
and be aware of shifts and their outcomes. It doesn't have to take long!

My Health	My Work	My Friends
My Children	**My Diet**	**My Dreams**
My Goals	**My Finances**	**My Partner**
My Family	**My Life**	**My Mental Health**

What's Happening Today __________

Track your moods or situations on a daily basis so that you can keep track of changes
and be aware of shifts and their outcomes. It doesn't have to take long!

My Health	My Work	My Friends

My Children	My Diet	My Dreams

My Goals	My Finances	My Partner

My Family	My Life	My Mental Health

What's Happening Today ___________

Track your moods or situations on a daily basis so that you can keep track of changes and be aware of shifts and their outcomes. It doesn't have to take long!

My Health	My Work	My Friends

My Children	My Diet	My Dreams

My Goals	My Finances	My Partner

My Family	My Life	My Mental Health

What's Happening Today __________

Track your moods or situations on a daily basis so that you can keep track of changes and be aware of shifts and their outcomes. It doesn't have to take long!

My Health	My Work	My Friends

My Children	My Diet	My Dreams

My Goals	My Finances	My Partner

My Family	My Life	My Mental Health

What's Happening Today ____________

Track your moods or situations on a daily basis so that you can keep track of changes
and be aware of shifts and their outcomes. It doesn't have to take long!

My Health	My Work	My Friends
My Children	My Diet	My Dreams
My Goals	My Finances	My Partner
My Family	My Life	My Mental Health

What's Happening Today _______________

Track your moods or situations on a daily basis so that you can keep track of changes
and be aware of shifts and their outcomes. It doesn't have to take long!

My Health	My Work	My Friends

My Children	My Diet	My Dreams

My Goals	My Finances	My Partner

My Family	My Life	My Mental Health

What's Happening Today __________

Track your moods or situations on a daily basis so that you can keep track of changes and be aware of shifts and their outcomes. It doesn't have to take long!

My Health	My Work	My Friends
My Children	My Diet	My Dreams
My Goals	My Finances	My Partner
My Family	My Life	My Mental Health

What's Happening Today ____________

Track your moods or situations on a daily basis so that you can keep track of changes and be aware of shifts and their outcomes. It doesn't have to take long!

My Health	My Work	My Friends

My Children	My Diet	My Dreams

My Goals	My Finances	My Partner

My Family	My Life	My Mental Health

What's Happening Today ___________

Track your moods or situations on a daily basis so that you can keep track of changes
and be aware of shifts and their outcomes. It doesn't have to take long!

My Health

My Work

My Friends

My Children

My Diet

My Dreams

My Goals

My Finances

My Partner

My Family

My Life

My Mental Health

What's Happening Today ____________

Track your moods or situations on a daily basis so that you can keep track of changes and be aware of shifts and their outcomes. It doesn't have to take long!

My Health	My Work	My Friends

My Children	My Diet	My Dreams

My Goals	My Finances	My Partner

My Family	My Life	My Mental Health

What's Happening Today _____________

Track your moods or situations on a daily basis so that you can keep track of changes
and be aware of shifts and their outcomes. It doesn't have to take long!

My Health	My Work	My Friends

My Children	My Diet	My Dreams

My Goals	My Finances	My Partner

My Family	My Life	My Mental Health

What's Happening Today __________

Track your moods or situations on a daily basis so that you can keep track of changes
and be aware of shifts and their outcomes. It doesn't have to take long!

My Health	My Work	My Friends

My Children	My Diet	My Dreams

My Goals	My Finances	My Partner

My Family	My Life	My Mental Health

What's Happening Today ___________

Track your moods or situations on a daily basis so that you can keep track of changes
and be aware of shifts and their outcomes. It doesn't have to take long!

My Health	My Work	My Friends
My Children	My Diet	My Dreams
My Goals	My Finances	My Partner
My Family	My Life	My Mental Health

What's Happening Today _________

Track your moods or situations on a daily basis so that you can keep track of changes and be aware of shifts and their outcomes. It doesn't have to take long!

My Health	My Work	My Friends
My Children	My Diet	My Dreams
My Goals	My Finances	My Partner
My Family	My Life	My Mental Health

What's Happening Today __________

Track your moods or situations on a daily basis so that you can keep track of changes and be aware of shifts and their outcomes. It doesn't have to take long!

My Health	My Work	My Friends

My Children	My Diet	My Dreams

My Goals	My Finances	My Partner

My Family	My Life	My Mental Health

What's Happening Today __________

Track your moods or situations on a daily basis so that you can keep track of changes and be aware of shifts and their outcomes. It doesn't have to take long!

My Health	My Work	My Friends
My Children	My Diet	My Dreams
My Goals	My Finances	My Partner
My Family	My Life	My Mental Health

What's Happening Today ___________

Track your moods or situations on a daily basis so that you can keep track of changes and be aware of shifts and their outcomes. It doesn't have to take long!

My Health	My Work	My Friends

My Children	My Diet	My Dreams

My Goals	My Finances	My Partner

My Family	My Life	My Mental Health

What's Happening Today _____________

Track your moods or situations on a daily basis so that you can keep track of changes
and be aware of shifts and their outcomes. It doesn't have to take long!

My Health	My Work	My Friends
My Children	**My Diet**	**My Dreams**
My Goals	**My Finances**	**My Partner**
My Family	**My Life**	**My Mental Health**

What's Happening Today ___________

Track your moods or situations on a daily basis so that you can keep track of changes
and be aware of shifts and their outcomes. It doesn't have to take long!

My Health	My Work	My Friends
My Children	My Diet	My Dreams
My Goals	My Finances	My Partner
My Family	My Life	My Mental Health

What's Happening Today _____________

Track your moods or situations on a daily basis so that you can keep track of changes
and be aware of shifts and their outcomes. It doesn't have to take long!

My Health	My Work	My Friends
My Children	**My Diet**	**My Dreams**
My Goals	**My Finances**	**My Partner**
My Family	**My Life**	**My Mental Health**

What's Happening Today ___________

Track your moods or situations on a daily basis so that you can keep track of changes
and be aware of shifts and their outcomes. It doesn't have to take long!

My Health	My Work	My Friends
My Children	**My Diet**	**My Dreams**
My Goals	**My Finances**	**My Partner**
My Family	**My Life**	**My Mental Health**

What's Happening Today ______________

Track your moods or situations on a daily basis so that you can keep track of changes and be aware of shifts and their outcomes. It doesn't have to take long!

My Health

My Work

My Friends

My Children

My Diet

My Dreams

My Goals

My Finances

My Partner

My Family

My Life

My Mental Health

What's Happening Today ___________

Track your moods or situations on a daily basis so that you can keep track of changes
and be aware of shifts and their outcomes. It doesn't have to take long!

My Health	My Work	My Friends
My Children	**My Diet**	**My Dreams**
My Goals	**My Finances**	**My Partner**
My Family	**My Life**	**My Mental Health**

What's Happening Today _____________

Track your moods or situations on a daily basis so that you can keep track of changes
and be aware of shifts and their outcomes. It doesn't have to take long!

My Health	My Work	My Friends

My Children	My Diet	My Dreams

My Goals	My Finances	My Partner

My Family	My Life	My Mental Health

What's Happening Today _____________

Track your moods or situations on a daily basis so that you can keep track of changes
and be aware of shifts and their outcomes. It doesn't have to take long!

My Health	My Work	My Friends
My Children	**My Diet**	**My Dreams**
My Goals	**My Finances**	**My Partner**
My Family	**My Life**	**My Mental Health**

What's Happening Today ____________

Track your moods or situations on a daily basis so that you can keep track of changes and be aware of shifts and their outcomes. It doesn't have to take long!

My Health	My Work	My Friends

My Children	My Diet	My Dreams

My Goals	My Finances	My Partner

My Family	My Life	My Mental Health

What's Happening Today _____________

Track your moods or situations on a daily basis so that you can keep track of changes
and be aware of shifts and their outcomes. It doesn't have to take long!

My Health	My Work	My Friends

My Children	My Diet	My Dreams

My Goals	My Finances	My Partner

My Family	My Life	My Mental Health

What's Happening Today _____________

Track your moods or situations on a daily basis so that you can keep track of changes
and be aware of shifts and their outcomes. It doesn't have to take long!

My Health	My Work	My Friends

My Children	My Diet	My Dreams

My Goals	My Finances	My Partner

My Family	My Life	My Mental Health

What's Happening Today _______________

Track your moods or situations on a daily basis so that you can keep track of changes
and be aware of shifts and their outcomes. It doesn't have to take long!

My Health	My Work	My Friends
My Children	**My Diet**	**My Dreams**
My Goals	**My Finances**	**My Partner**
My Family	**My Life**	**My Mental Health**

What's Happening Today _______________

Track your moods or situations on a daily basis so that you can keep track of changes
and be aware of shifts and their outcomes. It doesn't have to take long!

My Health	My Work	My Friends
My Children	**My Diet**	**My Dreams**
My Goals	**My Finances**	**My Partner**
My Family	**My Life**	**My Mental Health**

What's Happening Today _____________

My Health

My Work

My Friends

My Children

My Diet

My Dreams

My Goals

My Finances

My Partner

My Family

My Life

My Mental Health

What's Happening Today __________

Track your moods or situations on a daily basis so that you can keep track of changes
and be aware of shifts and their outcomes. It doesn't have to take long!

My Health	My Work	My Friends
My Children	My Diet	My Dreams
My Goals	My Finances	My Partner
My Family	My Life	My Mental Health

What's Happening Today _____________

Track your moods or situations on a daily basis so that you can keep track of changes and be aware of shifts and their outcomes. It doesn't have to take long!

My Health	My Work	My Friends
My Children	My Diet	My Dreams
My Goals	My Finances	My Partner
My Family	My Life	My Mental Health

What's Happening Today _____________

Track your moods or situations on a daily basis so that you can keep track of changes
and be aware of shifts and their outcomes. It doesn't have to take long!

My Health	**My Work**	**My Friends**
My Children	**My Diet**	**My Dreams**
My Goals	**My Finances**	**My Partner**
My Family	**My Life**	**My Mental Health**

What's Happening Today ___________

Track your moods or situations on a daily basis so that you can keep track of changes and be aware of shifts and their outcomes. It doesn't have to take long!

My Health	My Work	My Friends
My Children	My Diet	My Dreams
My Goals	My Finances	My Partner
My Family	My Life	My Mental Health

What's Happening Today __________

Track your moods or situations on a daily basis so that you can keep track of changes and be aware of shifts and their outcomes. It doesn't have to take long!

My Health	My Work	My Friends
My Children	My Diet	My Dreams
My Goals	My Finances	My Partner
My Family	My Life	My Mental Health

What's Happening Today _____________

Track your moods or situations on a daily basis so that you can keep track of changes and be aware of shifts and their outcomes. It doesn't have to take long!

My Health	My Work	My Friends
My Children	My Diet	My Dreams
My Goals	My Finances	My Partner
My Family	My Life	My Mental Health

What's Happening Today ___________

Track your moods or situations on a daily basis so that you can keep track of changes
and be aware of shifts and their outcomes. It doesn't have to take long!

My Health	My Work	My Friends

My Children	My Diet	My Dreams

My Goals	My Finances	My Partner

My Family	My Life	My Mental Health

What's Happening Today __________

Track your moods or situations on a daily basis so that you can keep track of changes
and be aware of shifts and their outcomes. It doesn't have to take long!

My Health	My Work	My Friends
My Children	My Diet	My Dreams
My Goals	My Finances	My Partner
My Family	My Life	My Mental Health

What's Happening Today ___________

Track your moods or situations on a daily basis so that you can keep track of changes
and be aware of shifts and their outcomes. It doesn't have to take long!

My Health

My Work

My Friends

My Children

My Diet

My Dreams

My Goals

My Finances

My Partner

My Family

My Life

My Mental Health

What's Happening Today _____________

Track your moods or situations on a daily basis so that you can keep track of changes and be aware of shifts and their outcomes. It doesn't have to take long!

My Health	My Work	My Friends
My Children	My Diet	My Dreams
My Goals	My Finances	My Partner
My Family	My Life	My Mental Health

What's Happening Today _____________

Track your moods or situations on a daily basis so that you can keep track of changes
and be aware of shifts and their outcomes. It doesn't have to take long!

My Health	My Work	My Friends

My Children	My Diet	My Dreams

My Goals	My Finances	My Partner

My Family	My Life	My Mental Health

What's Happening Today ___________

Track your moods or situations on a daily basis so that you can keep track of changes and be aware of shifts and their outcomes. It doesn't have to take long!

My Health	My Work	My Friends
My Children	My Diet	My Dreams
My Goals	My Finances	My Partner
My Family	My Life	My Mental Health

What's Happening Today _______________

Track your moods or situations on a daily basis so that you can keep track of changes
and be aware of shifts and their outcomes. It doesn't have to take long!

My Health	My Work	My Friends
My Children	**My Diet**	**My Dreams**
My Goals	**My Finances**	**My Partner**
My Family	**My Life**	**My Mental Health**

What's Happening Today __________

Track your moods or situations on a daily basis so that you can keep track of changes and be aware of shifts and their outcomes. It doesn't have to take long!

My Health	My Work	My Friends
My Children	My Diet	My Dreams
My Goals	My Finances	My Partner
My Family	My Life	My Mental Health

What's Happening Today ____________

Track your moods or situations on a daily basis so that you can keep track of changes
and be aware of shifts and their outcomes. It doesn't have to take long!

My Health	My Work	My Friends
My Children	**My Diet**	**My Dreams**
My Goals	**My Finances**	**My Partner**
My Family	**My Life**	**My Mental Health**

What's Happening Today __________

Track your moods or situations on a daily basis so that you can keep track of changes and be aware of shifts and their outcomes. It doesn't have to take long!

My Health	My Work	My Friends
My Children	**My Diet**	**My Dreams**
My Goals	**My Finances**	**My Partner**
My Family	**My Life**	**My Mental Health**

What's Happening Today _______________

Track your moods or situations on a daily basis so that you can keep track of changes
and be aware of shifts and their outcomes. It doesn't have to take long!

My Health	My Work	My Friends

My Children	My Diet	My Dreams

My Goals	My Finances	My Partner

My Family	My Life	My Mental Health

What's Happening Today ___________

Track your moods or situations on a daily basis so that you can keep track of changes
and be aware of shifts and their outcomes. It doesn't have to take long!

My Health	My Work	My Friends
My Children	My Diet	My Dreams
My Goals	My Finances	My Partner
My Family	My Life	My Mental Health

What's Happening Today _______________

Track your moods or situations on a daily basis so that you can keep track of changes
and be aware of shifts and their outcomes. It doesn't have to take long!

My Health	My Work	My Friends

My Children	My Diet	My Dreams

My Goals	My Finances	My Partner

My Family	My Life	My Mental Health

What's Happening Today __________

Track your moods or situations on a daily basis so that you can keep track of changes
and be aware of shifts and their outcomes. It doesn't have to take long!

My Health	My Work	My Friends
My Children	My Diet	My Dreams
My Goals	My Finances	My Partner
My Family	My Life	My Mental Health

What's Happening Today _____________

My Health	My Work	My Friends

My Children	My Diet	My Dreams

My Goals	My Finances	My Partner

My Family	My Life	My Mental Health

What's Happening Today _____________

Track your moods or situations on a daily basis so that you can keep track of changes and be aware of shifts and their outcomes. It doesn't have to take long!

My Health	My Work	My Friends
My Children	My Diet	My Dreams
My Goals	My Finances	My Partner
My Family	My Life	My Mental Health

What's Happening Today ____________

Track your moods or situations on a daily basis so that you can keep track of changes
and be aware of shifts and their outcomes. It doesn't have to take long!

My Health	My Work	My Friends
My Children	**My Diet**	**My Dreams**
My Goals	**My Finances**	**My Partner**
My Family	**My Life**	**My Mental Health**

What's Happening Today _____________

Track your moods or situations on a daily basis so that you can keep track of changes
and be aware of shifts and their outcomes. It doesn't have to take long!

My Health	My Work	My Friends

My Children	My Diet	My Dreams

My Goals	My Finances	My Partner

My Family	My Life	My Mental Health

What's Happening Today ___________

Track your moods or situations on a daily basis so that you can keep track of changes and be aware of shifts and their outcomes. It doesn't have to take long!

My Health	My Work	My Friends
My Children	My Diet	My Dreams
My Goals	My Finances	My Partner
My Family	My Life	My Mental Health

What's Happening Today ___________

Track your moods or situations on a daily basis so that you can keep track of changes and be aware of shifts and their outcomes. It doesn't have to take long!

My Health	My Work	My Friends

My Children	My Diet	My Dreams

My Goals	My Finances	My Partner

My Family	My Life	My Mental Health

What's Happening Today __________

Track your moods or situations on a daily basis so that you can keep track of changes and be aware of shifts and their outcomes. It doesn't have to take long!

My Health	My Work	My Friends

My Children	My Diet	My Dreams

My Goals	My Finances	My Partner

My Family	My Life	My Mental Health

What's Happening Today __________

My Health	My Work	My Friends
My Children	My Diet	My Dreams
My Goals	My Finances	My Partner
My Family	My Life	My Mental Health

What's Happening Today ___________

Track your moods or situations on a daily basis so that you can keep track of changes
and be aware of shifts and their outcomes. It doesn't have to take long!

My Health	My Work	My Friends
My Children	My Diet	My Dreams
My Goals	My Finances	My Partner
My Family	My Life	My Mental Health

What's Happening Today ____________

Track your moods or situations on a daily basis so that you can keep track of changes and be aware of shifts and their outcomes. It doesn't have to take long!

My Health	My Work	My Friends

My Children	My Diet	My Dreams

My Goals	My Finances	My Partner

My Family	My Life	My Mental Health

What's Happening Today __________

Track your moods or situations on a daily basis so that you can keep track of changes
and be aware of shifts and their outcomes. It doesn't have to take long!

My Health	My Work	My Friends

My Children	My Diet	My Dreams

My Goals	My Finances	My Partner

My Family	My Life	My Mental Health

What's Happening Today _______________

Track your moods or situations on a daily basis so that you can keep track of changes
and be aware of shifts and their outcomes. It doesn't have to take long!

My Health	My Work	My Friends
My Children	**My Diet**	**My Dreams**
My Goals	**My Finances**	**My Partner**
My Family	**My Life**	**My Mental Health**

What's Happening Today ____________

Track your moods or situations on a daily basis so that you can keep track of changes
and be aware of shifts and their outcomes. It doesn't have to take long!

My Health	My Work	My Friends

My Children	My Diet	My Dreams

My Goals	My Finances	My Partner

My Family	My Life	My Mental Health

What's Happening Today __________

Track your moods or situations on a daily basis so that you can keep track of changes
and be aware of shifts and their outcomes. It doesn't have to take long!

My Health	My Work	My Friends
My Children	My Diet	My Dreams
My Goals	My Finances	My Partner
My Family	My Life	My Mental Health

What's Happening Today __________

Track your moods or situations on a daily basis so that you can keep track of changes and be aware of shifts and their outcomes. It doesn't have to take long!

My Health	My Work	My Friends
My Children	My Diet	My Dreams
My Goals	My Finances	My Partner
My Family	My Life	My Mental Health

What's Happening Today __________

Track your moods or situations on a daily basis so that you can keep track of changes
and be aware of shifts and their outcomes. It doesn't have to take long!

My Health	My Work	My Friends
My Children	My Diet	My Dreams
My Goals	My Finances	My Partner
My Family	My Life	My Mental Health

What's Happening Today _____________

Track your moods or situations on a daily basis so that you can keep track of changes
and be aware of shifts and their outcomes. It doesn't have to take long!

My Health	My Work	My Friends
My Children	My Diet	My Dreams
My Goals	My Finances	My Partner
My Family	My Life	My Mental Health

What's Happening Today __________

Track your moods or situations on a daily basis so that you can keep track of changes
and be aware of shifts and their outcomes. It doesn't have to take long!

My Health	My Work	My Friends

My Children	My Diet	My Dreams

My Goals	My Finances	My Partner

My Family	My Life	My Mental Health

What's Happening Today _______________

Track your moods or situations on a daily basis so that you can keep track of changes and be aware of shifts and their outcomes. It doesn't have to take long!

My Health	My Work	My Friends
My Children	**My Diet**	**My Dreams**
My Goals	**My Finances**	**My Partner**
My Family	**My Life**	**My Mental Health**

What's Happening Today _____________

Track your moods or situations on a daily basis so that you can keep track of changes and be aware of shifts and their outcomes. It doesn't have to take long!

My Health	My Work	My Friends
My Children	My Diet	My Dreams
My Goals	My Finances	My Partner
My Family	My Life	My Mental Health

What's Happening Today ____________

Track your moods or situations on a daily basis so that you can keep track of changes
and be aware of shifts and their outcomes. It doesn't have to take long!

My Health	My Work	My Friends
My Children	**My Diet**	**My Dreams**
My Goals	**My Finances**	**My Partner**
My Family	**My Life**	**My Mental Health**

What's Happening Today _________

Track your moods or situations on a daily basis so that you can keep track of changes and be aware of shifts and their outcomes. It doesn't have to take long!

My Health	My Work	My Friends

My Children	My Diet	My Dreams

My Goals	My Finances	My Partner

My Family	My Life	My Mental Health

What's Happening Today __________

Track your moods or situations on a daily basis so that you can keep track of changes and be aware of shifts and their outcomes. It doesn't have to take long!

My Health	My Work	My Friends

My Children	My Diet	My Dreams

My Goals	My Finances	My Partner

My Family	My Life	My Mental Health

What's Happening Today _____________

Track your moods or situations on a daily basis so that you can keep track of changes
and be aware of shifts and their outcomes. It doesn't have to take long!

My Health	My Work	My Friends
My Children	**My Diet**	**My Dreams**
My Goals	**My Finances**	**My Partner**
My Family	**My Life**	**My Mental Health**

What's Happening Today __________

Track your moods or situations on a daily basis so that you can keep track of changes
and be aware of shifts and their outcomes. It doesn't have to take long!

My Health	My Work	My Friends
My Children	**My Diet**	**My Dreams**
My Goals	**My Finances**	**My Partner**
My Family	**My Life**	**My Mental Health**

What's Happening Today _____________

Track your moods or situations on a daily basis so that you can keep track of changes
and be aware of shifts and their outcomes. It doesn't have to take long!

My Health	My Work	My Friends

My Children	My Diet	My Dreams

My Goals	My Finances	My Partner

My Family	My Life	My Mental Health

What's Happening Today _____________

Track your moods or situations on a daily basis so that you can keep track of changes
and be aware of shifts and their outcomes. It doesn't have to take long!

My Health	My Work	My Friends
My Children	My Diet	My Dreams
My Goals	My Finances	My Partner
My Family	My Life	My Mental Health

What's Happening Today _____________

Track your moods or situations on a daily basis so that you can keep track of changes and be aware of shifts and their outcomes. It doesn't have to take long!

My Health	My Work	My Friends

My Children	My Diet	My Dreams

My Goals	My Finances	My Partner

My Family	My Life	My Mental Health

What's Happening Today _____________

Track your moods or situations on a daily basis so that you can keep track of changes
and be aware of shifts and their outcomes. It doesn't have to take long!

My Health	My Work	My Friends
My Children	My Diet	My Dreams
My Goals	My Finances	My Partner
My Family	My Life	My Mental Health

What's Happening Today _______________

Track your moods or situations on a daily basis so that you can keep track of changes and be aware of shifts and their outcomes. It doesn't have to take long!

My Health	My Work	My Friends
My Children	My Diet	My Dreams
My Goals	My Finances	My Partner
My Family	My Life	My Mental Health

What's Happening Today ___________

Track your moods or situations on a daily basis so that you can keep track of changes and be aware of shifts and their outcomes. It doesn't have to take long!

My Health	**My Work**	**My Friends**
My Children	**My Diet**	**My Dreams**
My Goals	**My Finances**	**My Partner**
My Family	**My Life**	**My Mental Health**

What's Happening Today ___________

Track your moods or situations on a daily basis so that you can keep track of changes and be aware of shifts and their outcomes. It doesn't have to take long!

My Health	My Work	My Friends
My Children	My Diet	My Dreams
My Goals	My Finances	My Partner
My Family	My Life	My Mental Health

What's Happening Today _______________

Track your moods or situations on a daily basis so that you can keep track of changes and be aware of shifts and their outcomes. It doesn't have to take long!

My Health	My Work	My Friends
My Children	My Diet	My Dreams
My Goals	My Finances	My Partner
My Family	My Life	My Mental Health

What's Happening Today _______________

Track your moods or situations on a daily basis so that you can keep track of changes
and be aware of shifts and their outcomes. It doesn't have to take long!

My Health	My Work	My Friends
My Children	My Diet	My Dreams
My Goals	My Finances	My Partner
My Family	My Life	My Mental Health

What's Happening Today __________

Track your moods or situations on a daily basis so that you can keep track of changes and be aware of shifts and their outcomes. It doesn't have to take long!

My Health	My Work	My Friends

My Children	My Diet	My Dreams

My Goals	My Finances	My Partner

My Family	My Life	My Mental Health

What's Happening Today __________

Track your moods or situations on a daily basis so that you can keep track of changes
and be aware of shifts and their outcomes. It doesn't have to take long!

My Health	My Work	My Friends
My Children	My Diet	My Dreams
My Goals	My Finances	My Partner
My Family	My Life	My Mental Health

What's Happening Today __________

Track your moods or situations on a daily basis so that you can keep track of changes
and be aware of shifts and their outcomes. It doesn't have to take long!

My Health	My Work	My Friends
My Children	**My Diet**	**My Dreams**
My Goals	**My Finances**	**My Partner**
My Family	**My Life**	**My Mental Health**

What's Happening Today __________

Track your moods or situations on a daily basis so that you can keep track of changes and be aware of shifts and their outcomes. It doesn't have to take long!

My Health	**My Work**	**My Friends**
My Children	**My Diet**	**My Dreams**
My Goals	**My Finances**	**My Partner**
My Family	**My Life**	**My Mental Health**

What's Happening Today ___________

Track your moods or situations on a daily basis so that you can keep track of changes and be aware of shifts and their outcomes. It doesn't have to take long!

My Health	My Work	My Friends
My Children	My Diet	My Dreams
My Goals	My Finances	My Partner
My Family	My Life	My Mental Health

What's Happening Today _____________

Track your moods or situations on a daily basis so that you can keep track of changes and be aware of shifts and their outcomes. It doesn't have to take long!

My Health	My Work	My Friends

My Children	My Diet	My Dreams

My Goals	My Finances	My Partner

My Family	My Life	My Mental Health

What's Happening Today _______________

Track your moods or situations on a daily basis so that you can keep track of changes
and be aware of shifts and their outcomes. It doesn't have to take long!

My Health	My Work	My Friends
My Children	**My Diet**	**My Dreams**
My Goals	**My Finances**	**My Partner**
My Family	**My Life**	**My Mental Health**

What's Happening Today _______________

Track your moods or situations on a daily basis so that you can keep track of changes and be aware of shifts and their outcomes. It doesn't have to take long!

My Health	My Work	My Friends
My Children	**My Diet**	**My Dreams**
My Goals	**My Finances**	**My Partner**
My Family	**My Life**	**My Mental Health**

What's Happening Today __________

Track your moods or situations on a daily basis so that you can keep track of changes and be aware of shifts and their outcomes. It doesn't have to take long!

My Health	My Work	My Friends
My Children	**My Diet**	**My Dreams**
My Goals	**My Finances**	**My Partner**
My Family	**My Life**	**My Mental Health**

What's Happening Today __________

Track your moods or situations on a daily basis so that you can keep track of changes and be aware of shifts and their outcomes. It doesn't have to take long!

My Health	My Work	My Friends
My Children	My Diet	My Dreams
My Goals	My Finances	My Partner
My Family	My Life	My Mental Health

What's Happening Today _______________

Track your moods or situations on a daily basis so that you can keep track of changes
and be aware of shifts and their outcomes. It doesn't have to take long!

My Health	My Work	My Friends
My Children	**My Diet**	**My Dreams**
My Goals	**My Finances**	**My Partner**
My Family	**My Life**	**My Mental Health**

What's Happening Today __________

Track your moods or situations on a daily basis so that you can keep track of changes
and be aware of shifts and their outcomes. It doesn't have to take long!

My Health	My Work	My Friends
My Children	**My Diet**	**My Dreams**
My Goals	**My Finances**	**My Partner**
My Family	**My Life**	**My Mental Health**

What's Happening Today __________

Track your moods or situations on a daily basis so that you can keep track of changes and be aware of shifts and their outcomes. It doesn't have to take long!

My Health	My Work	My Friends
My Children	**My Diet**	**My Dreams**
My Goals	**My Finances**	**My Partner**
My Family	**My Life**	**My Mental Health**

What's Happening Today __________

Track your moods or situations on a daily basis so that you can keep track of changes
and be aware of shifts and their outcomes. It doesn't have to take long!

My Health	My Work	My Friends
My Children	**My Diet**	**My Dreams**
My Goals	**My Finances**	**My Partner**
My Family	**My Life**	**My Mental Health**

What's Happening Today ___________

Track your moods or situations on a daily basis so that you can keep track of changes and be aware of shifts and their outcomes. It doesn't have to take long!

My Health	My Work	My Friends

My Children	My Diet	My Dreams

My Goals	My Finances	My Partner

My Family	My Life	My Mental Health

What's Happening Today __________

Track your moods or situations on a daily basis so that you can keep track of changes
and be aware of shifts and their outcomes. It doesn't have to take long!

My Health	My Work	My Friends
My Children	**My Diet**	**My Dreams**
My Goals	**My Finances**	**My Partner**
My Family	**My Life**	**My Mental Health**

What's Happening Today __________

Track your moods or situations on a daily basis so that you can keep track of changes and be aware of shifts and their outcomes. It doesn't have to take long!

My Health	My Work	My Friends
My Children	My Diet	My Dreams
My Goals	My Finances	My Partner
My Family	My Life	My Mental Health

What's Happening Today _____________

Track your moods or situations on a daily basis so that you can keep track of changes and be aware of shifts and their outcomes. It doesn't have to take long!

My Health	My Work	My Friends
My Children	**My Diet**	**My Dreams**
My Goals	**My Finances**	**My Partner**
My Family	**My Life**	**My Mental Health**

What's Happening Today __________

Track your moods or situations on a daily basis so that you can keep track of changes
and be aware of shifts and their outcomes. It doesn't have to take long!

My Health	My Work	My Friends

My Children	My Diet	My Dreams

My Goals	My Finances	My Partner

My Family	My Life	My Mental Health

What's Happening Today _____________

My Health	My Work	My Friends
My Children	My Diet	My Dreams
My Goals	My Finances	My Partner
My Family	My Life	My Mental Health

What's Happening Today __________

Track your moods or situations on a daily basis so that you can keep track of changes and be aware of shifts and their outcomes. It doesn't have to take long!

My Health	My Work	My Friends

My Children	My Diet	My Dreams

My Goals	My Finances	My Partner

My Family	My Life	My Mental Health

What's Happening Today __________

Track your moods or situations on a daily basis so that you can keep track of changes and be aware of shifts and their outcomes. It doesn't have to take long!

My Health	My Work	My Friends

My Children	My Diet	My Dreams

My Goals	My Finances	My Partner

My Family	My Life	My Mental Health

What's Happening Today _______________

My Health	My Work	My Friends
My Children	**My Diet**	**My Dreams**
My Goals	**My Finances**	**My Partner**
My Family	**My Life**	**My Mental Health**

What's Happening Today _____________

Track your moods or situations on a daily basis so that you can keep track of changes and be aware of shifts and their outcomes. It doesn't have to take long!

My Health	My Work	My Friends
My Children	My Diet	My Dreams
My Goals	My Finances	My Partner
My Family	My Life	My Mental Health

What's Happening Today __________

Track your moods or situations on a daily basis so that you can keep track of changes
and be aware of shifts and their outcomes. It doesn't have to take long!

My Health	My Work	My Friends
My Children	My Diet	My Dreams
My Goals	My Finances	My Partner
My Family	My Life	My Mental Health

What's Happening Today __________

Track your moods or situations on a daily basis so that you can keep track of changes
and be aware of shifts and their outcomes. It doesn't have to take long!

My Health	My Work	My Friends
My Children	**My Diet**	**My Dreams**
My Goals	**My Finances**	**My Partner**
My Family	**My Life**	**My Mental Health**

What's Happening Today __________

Track your moods or situations on a daily basis so that you can keep track of changes and be aware of shifts and their outcomes. It doesn't have to take long!

My Health	My Work	My Friends
My Children	My Diet	My Dreams
My Goals	My Finances	My Partner
My Family	My Life	My Mental Health

What's Happening Today __________

Track your moods or situations on a daily basis so that you can keep track of changes
and be aware of shifts and their outcomes. It doesn't have to take long!

My Health	My Work	My Friends

My Children	My Diet	My Dreams

My Goals	My Finances	My Partner

My Family	My Life	My Mental Health

What's Happening Today __________

Track your moods or situations on a daily basis so that you can keep track of changes and be aware of shifts and their outcomes. It doesn't have to take long!

My Health	My Work	My Friends
My Children	My Diet	My Dreams
My Goals	My Finances	My Partner
My Family	My Life	My Mental Health

What's Happening Today _____________

Track your moods or situations on a daily basis so that you can keep track of changes
and be aware of shifts and their outcomes. It doesn't have to take long!

My Health	My Work	My Friends
My Children	My Diet	My Dreams
My Goals	My Finances	My Partner
My Family	My Life	My Mental Health

What's Happening Today __________

Track your moods or situations on a daily basis so that you can keep track of changes
and be aware of shifts and their outcomes. It doesn't have to take long!

My Health	My Work	My Friends

My Children	My Diet	My Dreams

My Goals	My Finances	My Partner

My Family	My Life	My Mental Health

What's Happening Today __________

Track your moods or situations on a daily basis so that you can keep track of changes and be aware of shifts and their outcomes. It doesn't have to take long!

My Health

My Work

My Friends

My Children

My Diet

My Dreams

My Goals

My Finances

My Partner

My Family

My Life

My Mental Health